HOW TOILETS WORK

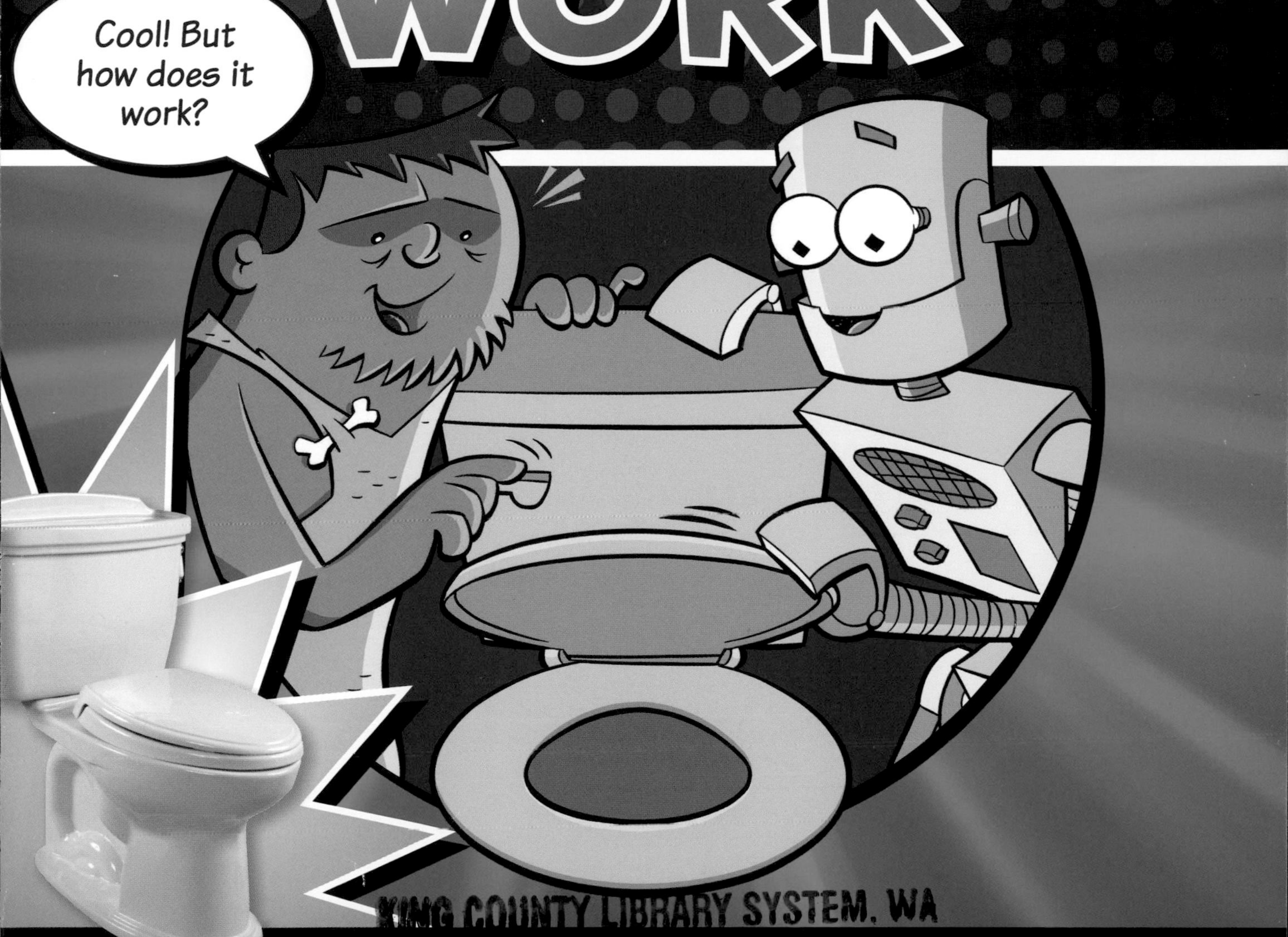

The Child's World®

Published by The Child's World®
1980 Lookout Drive • Mankato, MN 56003-1705
800-599-READ • www.childsworld.com

ACKNOWLEDGMENTS
The Child's World®: Mary Berendes, Publishing Director
Content Consultant: Paul Ohmann, PhD, Associate Professor
 of Physics, University of St. Thomas
The Design Lab: Design and production
Red Line Editorial: Editorial direction

LIBRARY OF CONGRESS
CATALOGING-IN-PUBLICATION DATA
Jacobson, Ryan.
  How toilets work / by Ryan Jacobson ;
illlustrated by Glen Mullaly.
     p. cm.
  Includes bibliographical references and index.
  ISBN 978-1-60973-223-3 (library reinforced : alk. paper)
  I. Toilets—Juvenile literature. I. Mullaly, Glen, 1968- ill. II.
Title.
  TH6498.J33 2011
  696'.182—dc23   2011013788

Photo Credits © Fotolia, cover, 1, 11, 27 (bottom right),
30; Simon Gurney/iStockphoto, 6; Ermin Gutenberger/
iStockphoto, 7; Ivan Cholakov/iStockphoto, 19; Adrian
Beesley/iStockphoto, 24; iStockphoto, 25 (bottom left), 27
(bottom left); Tanya Costey/iStockphoto, 25 (bottom right);
The Meyer-Sniffen Co./Library of Congress, 26 (bottom left);
Vigouroux Frédéric/iStockphoto, 26 (bottom right); Michael
Guttman/iStockphoto, 26 (top)

Printed in the United States of America in Mankato,
Minnesota.
July 2011
PA02092

ABOUT THE AUTHOR
Ryan Jacobson is a successful author
and presenter. He has written nearly 20
children's books—including picture books,
graphic novels, chapter books and choose-
your-path books—with several more
projects in the works. He has presented
at dozens of schools, organizations,
and special events. Ryan lives in Mora,
Minnesota, with his wife Lora, sons Jonah
and Lucas, and dog Boo. For more about
the author, please visit his website at
www.RyanJacobsonOnline.com.

ABOUT THE ILLUSTRATOR
Glen Mullaly draws neato pictures for kids
of all ages from his swanky studio on the
west coast of Canada. He lives with his
awesomely understanding wife and their
spectacularly indifferent cat. Glen loves
old books, magazines, and cartoons, and
someday wants to illustrate a book on How
Monsters Work!

TABLE OF CONTENTS

CHAPTER ONE

LET ME IN!

It's a steamy summer day. You break a sweat just opening your front door. Your flip-flops practically sizzle on the sidewalk. You think about flinging a Frisbee but you don't have the energy to even lift your wrist.

Forget it. You find a shady spot to chill. "Honey Bear, want a nice, cold drink?" your mom asks. Soon, there's with a frosted pitcher on the grass by your side.

You didn't realize how thirsty you were! You have one lemonade, then another, then a third. Then you suck on the ice on the bottom. Ahhhhh . . .

Hmmmm. You put it off for as long as you can, but finally, it's time to move. *You've got to go*.

You hurry inside to the bathroom door. You twist the knob and push. It doesn't budge! From the other side, you hear your sister's whiny voice. "I'm already in here."

Oh, no! It's a disaster . . . but it could be worse. What if you didn't have a toilet at all?

History describes many different ways people "went to the bathroom." Some are interesting—others are disgusting! Let's take a quick look at toilets over the years.

Sewer systems were being developed across the United States, but most people still had to use outhouses. These backyard shacks featured a toilet seat built over a deep hole in the ground. Very soon, however, indoor toilets became widely used.

Ancient Romans developed a sewer system. People dumped their waste into the streets. When the streets got washed, the waste flowed into the sewers. These poured into nearby rivers and streams. By about 100 years later, Roman homes were connected to pipes that carried waste directly into the sewer system.

This ancient bridge was built by the Romans as part of their sewer system.

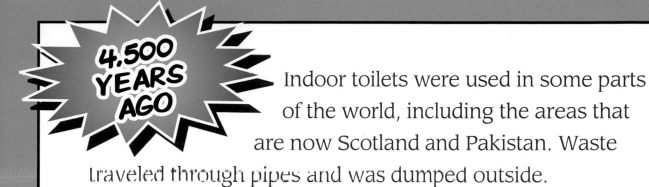

4,500 YEARS AGO Indoor toilets were used in some parts of the world, including the areas that are now Scotland and Pakistan. Waste traveled through pipes and was dumped outside.

BACK TO TODAY In the United States, almost every home has at least one toilet. But around the world, 2.6 billion people do not have access to safe, clean toilets and sewer systems. Many countries are working together to reduce this problem by the year 2015.

HISTORY STINKS!

Check out these fun-to-know facts about the history of toilets:

- The world's first known flush toilet was built in Crete more than 4,000 years ago. The island's royal palace bathroom had a large tank on its roof. The tank caught and stored rainwater. Inside was a toilet made of a wooden seat and a pan. After using it, a palace guest could flush using the stored rainwater.

- In Rome, early toilets were built in public, without walls. Men and women shared the toilets. They went to the bathroom in the open. Sometimes they even held meetings while sitting on the toilets!

Why is my face on the bottom of this chamber pot?

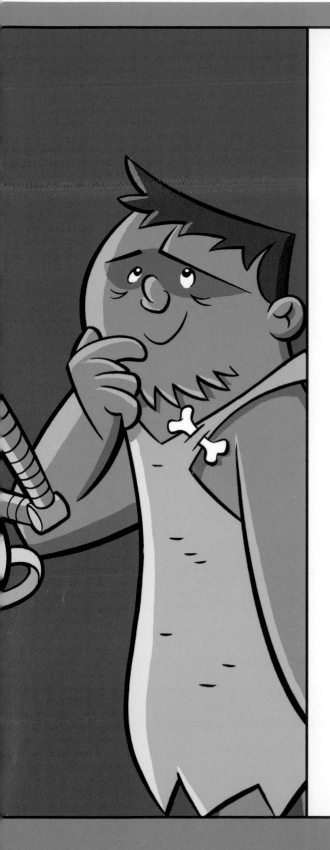

- During the Middle Ages, about 1,000 years ago, castles used garderobes. These were toilet-like seats built into tiny rooms. The rooms stuck out of the castle and hung over the moat. Waste from the garderobes dropped directly into the smelly moat water.

- In early America, many people went to the bathroom in little pots that could be dumped out a door or window. These were called **chamber pots**. Some chamber pots were made with the face of a disliked person painted on the bottom. People would go right on that face!

- In 1858, the rivers around London, England, became clogged with human waste, dead animals, and garbage. This caused "the Great Stink." The city smelled so bad that some people left town for months. They didn't come back until the problem was fixed and the smell went away.

WIPE OUT!

Modern toilet paper has been sold for about 150 years, but people were using toilets long before that. What did people use to wipe before toilet paper? The simple answer is . . . anything they could find. That included rocks, sand, pinecones, leaves, books—you name it. Sometimes, people even used their bare hands.

In ancient Rome, the citizens used a sea sponge attached to a long stick. They rinsed the sponge in water, cleaned themselves with it, and rinsed it again. Then they left it for the next person.

A favorite early "toilet paper" in the United States was corncobs. Baskets of corncobs were kept near toilets for wiping.

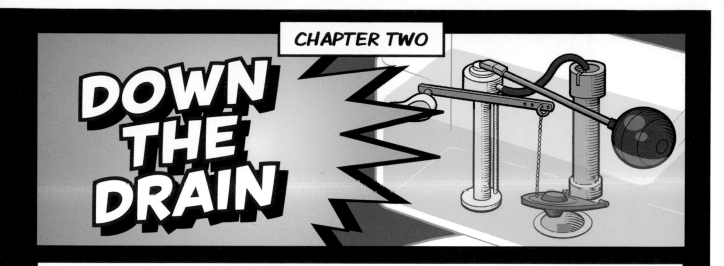

CHAPTER TWO

DOWN THE DRAIN

Raise your hand if you think toilets are gross. Now raise your hand if you'd rather go without one. No way! Almost every home in America has a toilet, and some have several. But have you ever wondered what happens when you flush? The flushing of a toilet can be divided into three parts. Let's take a look at each, one by one.

1. THE FLUSH

So what's the next step after using the toilet? You reach out, touch the handle, and—*whooosh*. This begins a series of events that happen inside the toilet's tank.

Have you ever peeked inside a toilet tank? Then you know it's filled with water—usually about three or four gallons (11 to 15 liters). To make the toilet flush, this water needs to get down into the bowl. You've already begun that process by pressing on the handle.

Inside the tank, a chain attaches the handle to a flap. When you press the handle down, it pulls on the chain, lifting the flap. Below the flap is a drain hole. Water empties from the tank and rushes into the bowl.

All of this happens in about three seconds, and it begins the second part of the flushing process.

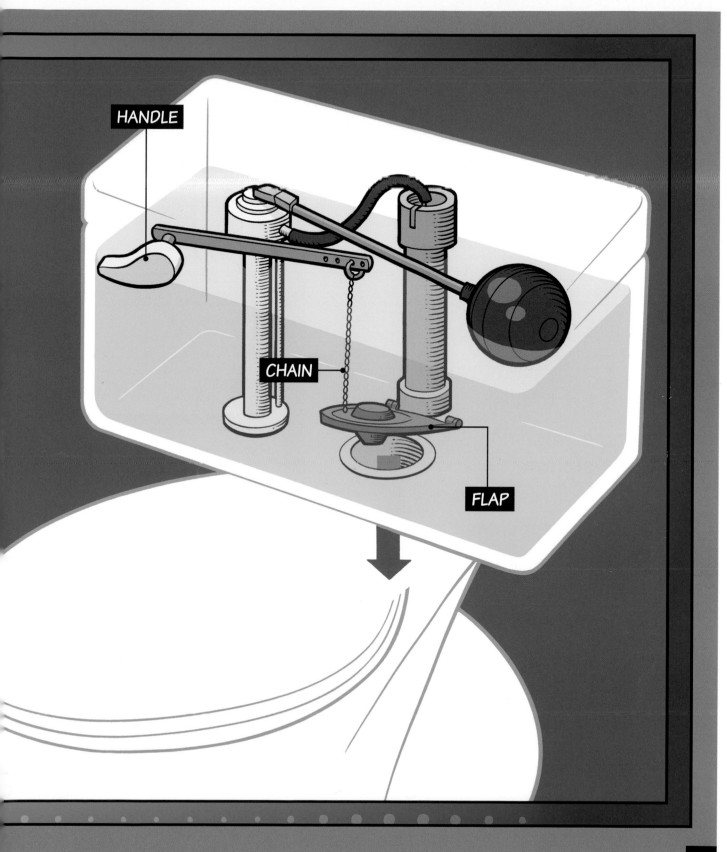

HANDLE

CHAIN

FLAP

You probably have an idea about what happens next. You can see this step happening in the toilet bowl. But did you know that the key to flushing rests on a part called the bowl **siphon**?

It sounds like a fancy, expensive piece of equipment. But the siphon is really just a tube below the bowl. It was molded into the toilet when the toilet was first made.

SIPHON

How does a siphon work? At first, a toilet's water level stays just below the point where the siphon begins to loop downward. As long as the water level stays here, the toilet will not flush.

But when you add enough water to fill the siphon at a fast-enough speed, the result is amazing. With a little help from gravity, the siphon sucks everything out of the bowl. Then it sends it down the sewer pipe.

The siphon doesn't stop sucking until most of the water is gone. That's when you hear your toilet make its famous gurgling sound.

DO IT YOURSELF

You can flush your toilet without ever touching the handle. Just dump a bucket of water into the toilet bowl.

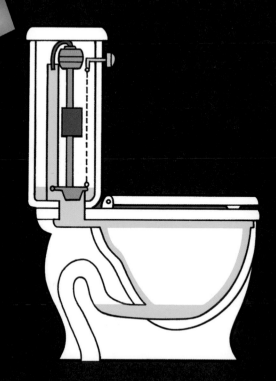

3. THE REFILL

You'll want your toilet to work again the next time you use it, right? Well, we just learned that the siphon needs water from the tank to flush. So now the tank fills itself again.

When the tank is empty, the flap falls back into place. It covers the drain hole. Now the tank is ready to be refilled.

Like a faucet, a valve inside the tank turns the flow of water on and off. The valve is connected to a float ball. This floats on the water when the water is high in the tank. When the tank empties, the float ball lowers. That turns the valve—and the water—on.

The water flows in two directions. Some travels through a tube and refills the toilet bowl. The rest goes into the tank.

As the tank fills, the float ball rises. Eventually, it floats high enough to turn the valve off. This stops the flow of water. Now the toilet is ready for the next person who needs it.

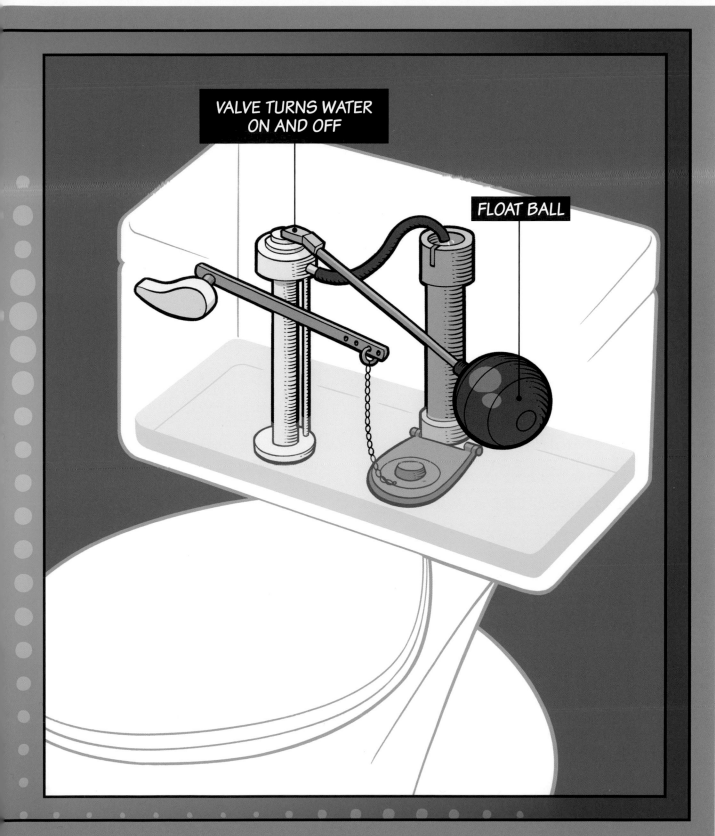

VALVE TURNS WATER
ON AND OFF

FLOAT BALL

CHAPTER THREE

BUT WHAT HAPPENS NEXT?

Okay, the toilet's been flushed. The waste went down the drain. But where does it go from there?

The answer depends on where you are. If you live in an area with few people, your family might have a **septic tank**. (See pages 22–23.) Most people who live in towns and cities share a wastewater, or sewage, system.

The toilet and other drains in your house connect to an underground pipe. This links to a larger underground pipe, called a **sewer main**. Often, sewer mains run beneath city streets. One might run below the street in front of your house.

Sewer mains connect and flow into bigger and bigger pipes. They bring all of the area's waste—including yours—to a wastewater treatment plant. The plant is

almost always built where the ground is lower than the city. This way, the pipes can slope downward from people's homes all the way to the plant.

MANHOLE COVERS

You can tell if a sewer main runs below your street by checking for manhole covers. Beneath each heavy, round lid is a shaft that leads down to the sewer main. Manholes allow workers to gain access to the sewers, just in case something needs to be checked or fixed.

WASTEWATER TREATMENT PLANT

When sewage reaches the wastewater treatment plant, it goes through several steps before it's clean.

SCREENS

SETTLING POOLS

SCUM

WATER

SLUDGE

1. Wastewater flows through a screen and into a series of pools.

2. Here, the wastewater separates into three layers. Solid waste, or sludge, falls to the bottom. Floating waste, or scum, rises to the top. The middle layer is water.

3. As the layer of water continues on, the scum and sludge is left behind. This waste is collected and either dumped into a landfill, used as fertilizer for growing plants, or burned up.

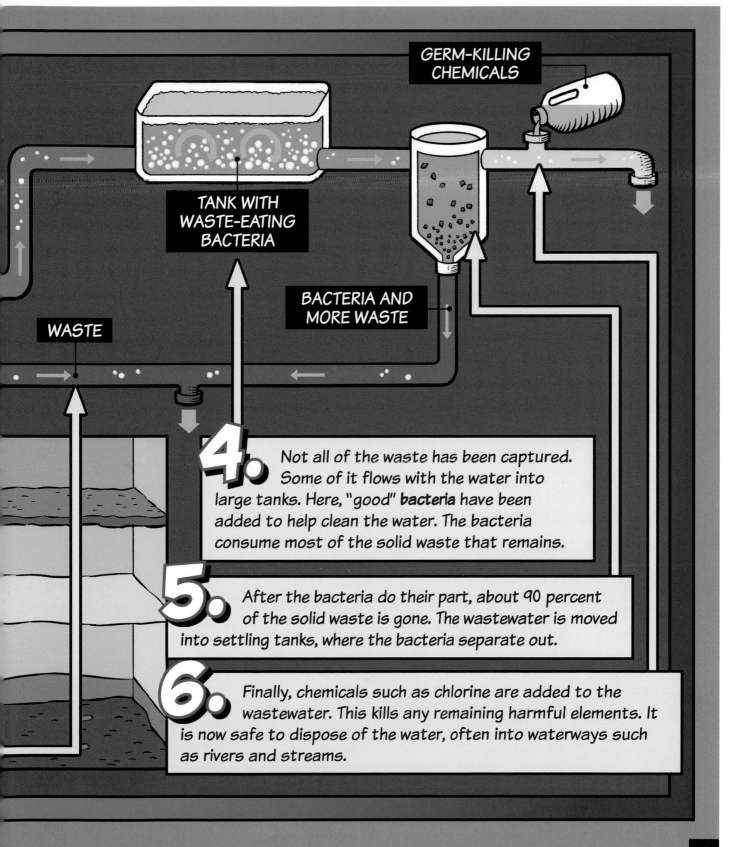

GERM-KILLING CHEMICALS

TANK WITH WASTE-EATING BACTERIA

BACTERIA AND MORE WASTE

WASTE

4. Not all of the waste has been captured. Some of it flows with the water into large tanks. Here, "good" **bacteria** have been added to help clean the water. The bacteria consume most of the solid waste that remains.

5. After the bacteria do their part, about 90 percent of the solid waste is gone. The wastewater is moved into settling tanks, where the bacteria separate out.

6. Finally, chemicals such as chlorine are added to the wastewater. This kills any remaining harmful elements. It is now safe to dispose of the water, often into waterways such as rivers and streams.

TANK YOU VERY MUCH

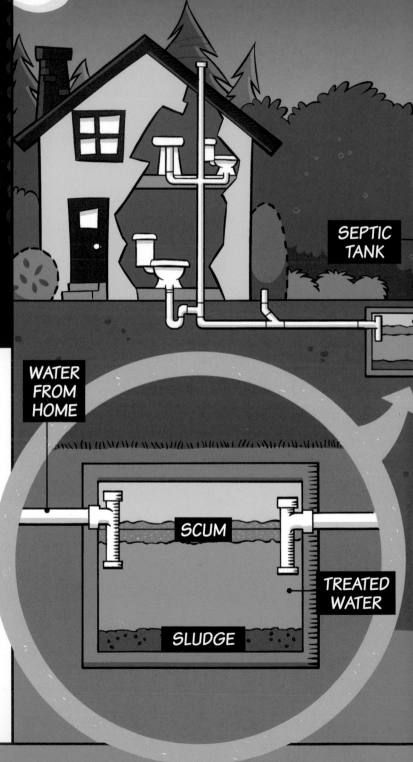

SEPTIC TANK

WATER FROM HOME

SCUM

TREATED WATER

SLUDGE

Some people's homes aren't connected to wastewater treatment plants. They often have their own sewage systems—right under their property. The central part of such a system is the septic tank. This large tank can hold more than 1,000 gallons (3,785 liters) of water.

DRAIN FIELD

Wastewater flowing from the house moves directly through an underground pipe and into the septic tank. Here, it divides into three layers: the scum layer at the top, the sludge layer at the bottom, and the water layer in between. The water in the tank is treated with chemicals and bacteria.

What happens when the septic tank is full? When wastewater from the house flows into the full tank, it pushes treated water out through another pipe. This "safe" water travels to a **drain field**. Here, the water slowly seeps into the earth.

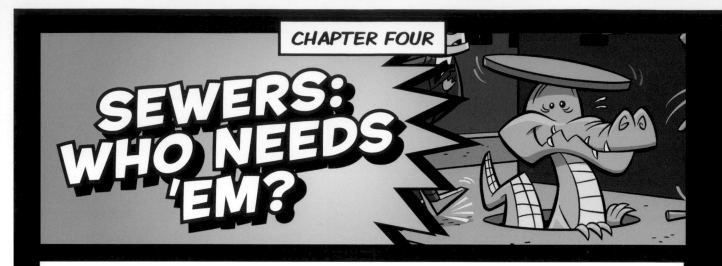

CHAPTER FOUR

SEWERS: WHO NEEDS 'EM?

Wow, underground pipes, chemicals, bacteria, septic tanks—the whole process sounds like a lot of trouble. Why do we even bother?

Here are three good reasons for handling sewage with care.

1. Sewage stinks.

Imagine everyone in your school going to the bathroom and then throwing it out the window. It wouldn't take

TIME LINE

ABOUT 2800 BC
Toilets are used in some parts of the world.

ABOUT 2500 BC
Flush toilets and a drainage system are used in what is now Pakistan.

ABOUT 2000 BC
A sewer system is developed on the island of Crete.

ABOUT 1000 BC
Citizens of the ancient Greek city of Ephesus share public toilets.

long for the entire schoolyard—and the entire school—to smell like a dirty toilet. Now, if everyone in the world did that . . . yuck.

> Sometimes I'm really glad I'm not human.

2. Sewage is dangerous.

Human waste is filled with bacteria. It can make people sick—and worse. In 1885, heavy rain in Chicago caused sewage to flow into the city's drinking water. The resulting diseases caused nearly 12 percent of Chicago residents to die.

ABOUT 500 AD
Chamber pots and garderobes are more common than toilets.

1391
Modern toilet paper is invented in China.

1596
The "modern" flush toilet is invented.

1857
Toilet paper is first sold in the United States.

3. Sewage is bad for Earth.

When untreated sewage gets into lakes and rivers, the bacteria harms the water. Oxygen levels in the water go down, killing fish, frogs, and other wild animals.

1858
The Great Stink occurs in London, England.

1884
Thomas Crapper designs a better flush system and begins selling toilets.

1890s
Most cities begin using special chemicals to treat waste.

EARLY 1900s
The modern system for treating waste with bacteria is developed.

A TALL TALE

As the story goes, alligators—some of them mutant giants—live in our sewers. Where did this false story come from? It is said to have started in 1935, when a captured alligator fell off a boat and into a New York City river. The gator escaped and was later found in the city's sewer system. After that, storytellers went wild, and the tall tale got bigger and bigger.

1935 TO 1943
Teams of men build thousands of outhouses as part of the US Works Progress Administration.

2008
The United Nations sponsors the International Year of Sanitation.

TODAY
You'll find at least one toilet in almost every home in the United States.

CHAPTER FIVE

A WORLD OF WORK TO DO

Not everyone in the world is as lucky as we are. Believe it or not, 2.6 billion people don't have good enough toilets and sewer systems. Most of these people live in poorer parts of Africa or Asia.

In these parts of the world, human waste mixes with nearby sources of drinking water. Many people, especially babies and children, get sick. More than 5,000 children die every day because of poor **sanitation**.

But the rest of the world isn't just standing by and letting this happen. The United Nations declared 2008 the International Year of Sanitation to draw attention to the issue. They made a goal to drastically reduce the world's sanitation problems by 2015. By that year, they want to halve the number of people on the planet who don't have

November 19 is World Toilet Day. It's a day to celebrate the importance of good sanitation. It's also a day to remember those less fortunate than we are. Around the world, diarrhea is the leading cause of illness and death—and poor sanitation is the main reason for it.

access to clean toilets and effective sewer systems. It's a big goal, and it will cost an average of $10 billion per year. But it's a mission that will save countless lives.

TOILET TANK TRICK

While almost a billion people around the world don't have clean water to drink, most of the toilets in America flush good water down the drain. In fact, some toilets use up to five gallons (19 liters) more water than needed—per flush!

Did you know there's a simple trick that can help your toilet save water? All you need is a little bit of sand, a plastic water or soda bottle, and an adult's help. Just have the adult take the cover off your toilet's tank. Put sand in the bottom of the bottle and fill the rest of the bottle with water. Screw a cap onto the bottle and set it in a corner of the tank, away from any of the parts inside. (If there's room, you might even want to add a second bottle.) Your adult helper can replace the tank lid, and you're done.

And what did you just do? You've made your toilet tank "smaller." It takes less water to fill it up. That can save up to 10 gallons (38 liters) of water every day! Tell your parents to buy you something nice with the money they'll save.

DRINK TO THE FUTURE!

What will the toilets of tomorrow be like? We can find hints in the toilets of today, which use less and less water with every flush. Saving water is key, and there is perhaps no better example of this than the toilet-to-tap system. We've already learned that treated water is "safe." The toilet-to-tap system takes this one step further. It turns wastewater into drinking water.

Are you grossed out? Don't be. A few US cities already use this system, as do astronauts. Someday, the toilet-to-tap system will likely be as common to us as dumping waste into the streets was 2,000 years ago.

That's not what they mean by recycling wastewater.

WORDS TO KNOW

bacteria (bak-TIHR-ee-uh): Bacteria are organisms that are so small they can be seen only with a microscope. Certain kinds of bacteria can be used to treat wastewater.

chamber pot (CHAYM-buhr POT): A chamber pot was a small pot that people used for going to the bathroom in past centuries. The waste from a chamber pot was dumped out a door or window.

drain field (DRAYN FEELD): A drain field is an underground trench used with a septic tank. In a drain field, treated wastewater slowly seeps into the ground.

landfill (LAND-fihl): A landfill is a site where garbage gets dumped and buried. Sludge from wastewater treatment may end up in a landfill.

sanitation (SAN-uh-TAY-shuhn): Sanitation refers to general health conditions. One way to improve sanitation is by making sure people have access to toilets.

septic tank (SEHP-tik TANGK): A septic tank is the central part of an individual home's wastewater system. Inside a septic tank, wastewater is treated so it can be absorbed by the surrounding earth.

sewer main (SOO-uhr MAYN): A sewer main is a large pipe that connects a home's drain pipes to the pipes leading into a wastewater plant. A sewer main usually runs under the street.

siphon (SY-fun): A siphon is a tube that pulls liquid down with the help of gravity. A siphon is a key part of a flushing toilet.

INDEX

FIND OUT MORE

Visit our Web site for links about how toilets work: childsworld.com/links

Note to Parents, Teachers, and Librarians: We routinely verify our Web links to make sure they are safe and active sites. So encourage your readers to check them out!